In the Middle of the Night

by Joy Cowley

It was a quiet night on the farm.
The moon was bright,
the stars were out,
and the old dog was thirsty.

She went to the watering can
for a drink.

Unfortunately,
her head got stuck in the can.
The old dog howled
and bashed the watering can
against the shed.

The noise woke up the first farmer.
He tiptoed to the window.

In the moonlight,
he saw a strange sight.

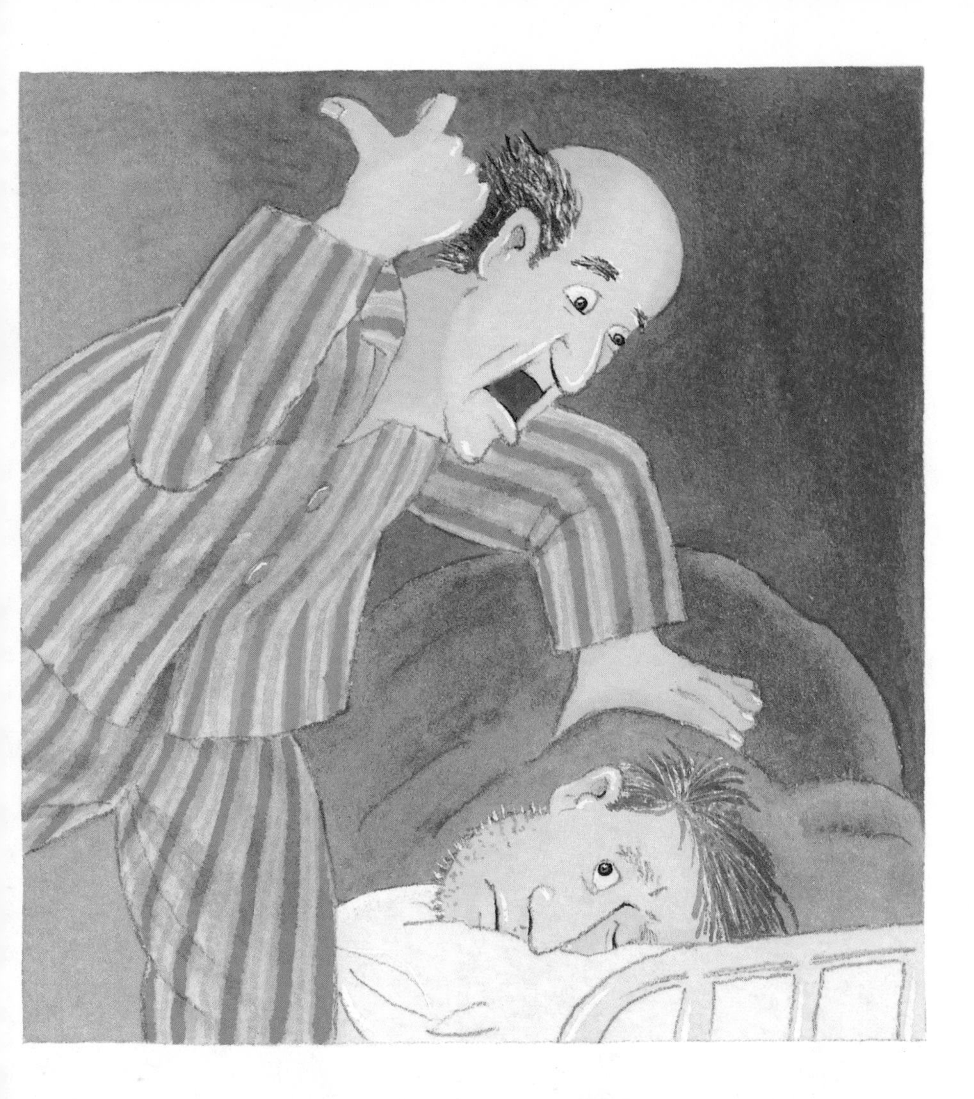

He shook the second farmer.
"Wake up! Wake up!
A thing with a big head
is attacking our shed!"

The second farmer got such a fright, he fell out of bed.

He ran to the third farmer.
"Get up! Get up!
A big monster is attacking us!"

The third farmer jumped out of bed and ran to wake the fourth farmer.

"Get up at once!" she shouted. "We're being attacked by monsters from outer space!"

The fourth farmer
ran to tell the fifth farmer.

"Monsters from outer space
have landed on the farm.
They're going to take over the world!"

The five farmers dressed so quickly, they put their clothes on backwards.

The first farmer grabbed the car keys. "Let's get out of here!"

"Wait a minute!"
said the fifth farmer.
"We can't leave the old dog behind.
The monsters might get her!"

The brave fifth farmer went outside.
He came back with the old dog.

"Poor old thing," he said.
"She was so scared of the monsters,
she was trying to hide
in the watering can!"

Then the five farmers
and the old dog
got in the car and drove away
as fast as they could,
to tell the rest of the world
about the monsters
from outer space.

Once more,
it was a quiet night on the farm.